Laughter Is The Best Exercise

by SCHULZ

HarperCollins*Publishers*

Escaping
Aerobics

NOW, JUST RELAX YOUR BREATHING, AND LET ALL THE TENSION GO OUT OF YOUR BODY...

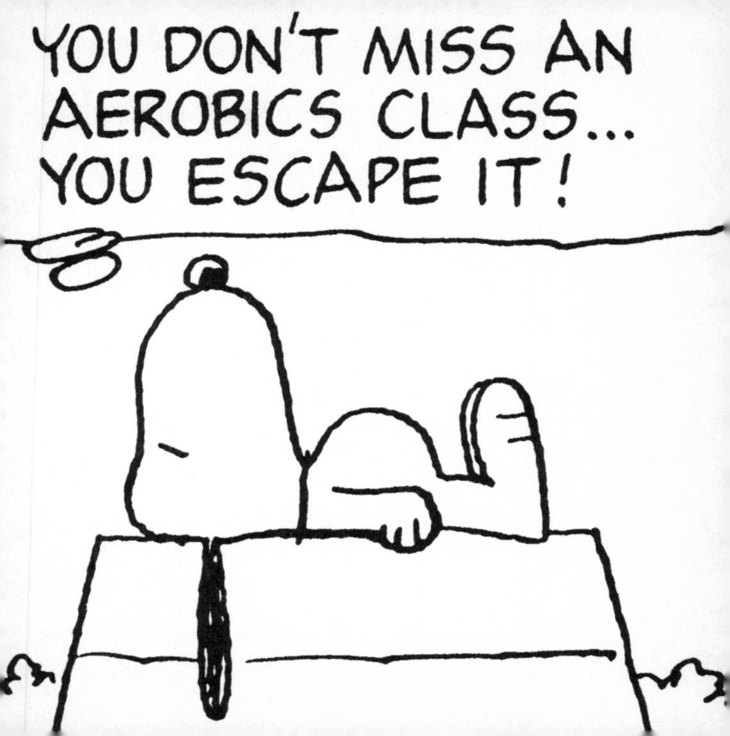
YOU DON'T MISS AN AEROBICS CLASS...
YOU ESCAPE IT!

Sit
&
Get Fit

Crash Diets
&
Power Doughnuts

WHATEVER HAPPENED TO SUPPER AROUND THE OL' KITCHEN TABLE?

HarperCollins*Publishers*

Produced by Jennifer Barry Design, Sausalito, CA
Creative consultation by 360°, NYC.
First published in 1997 by HarperCollins*Publishers* Inc.
http://www.harpercollins.com

ISBN 0-06-757454-8

Printed in Hong Kong

1 3 5 7 9 10 8 6 4 2